OXFORD POETS 2000

Oxford*Poets* 2000

an anthology edited by
*David Constantine, Hermione Lee
and Bernard O'Donoghue*

Oxford*Poets*

CARCANET

First published in Great Britain in 2000 by
Carcanet Press Limited
4th Floor, Conavon Court
12–16 Blackfriars Street
Manchester M3 5BQ

A CIP catalogue record for this book
is available from the British Library
ISBN 1 903 039 03 7

The publisher acknowledges financial assistance
from the Arts Council of England

Set in 10pt Bembo by XL Publishing Services, Tiverton
Printed and bound in England by SRP Ltd, Exeter

CONTENTS

Joe Sheerin

Sue Hubbard

STEPHANIE NORGATE

Mrs Rochester

When he's sent Grace away, he likes
to snuff the candle with his fingers,
wave away the burning wax smell of it
a priest in this dark musty church.

He lies down with me on the mattress
he heaved up here alone. At first,
he came for sleep but now he undresses my breasts,
fingering my nipples, gasping, making me gasp.

I have draped the roof-room in leftover white lace,
big fancy swathes of it. I am his virgin,
just like the games we used to play.
When he pushes in, he calls out 'Jane, Jane'
missing her. If I could bleed for him,
I would. I'll rub against him later,
when he sleeps, to get my pleasure.
Whose name shall I call?

The morning after, like a good wife, I'll watch him
from the attic window, riding out,
relieved, the spark back in his eye.

And there are nights
when I study him, light every line
of his face with the candle. He'll wake
terrified at my big trembling shadow.
'What do you want?' he'll cry.
His terror angers me. All I want to do
is light his face with the flame.
He holds my arms, fights me,
pushing me back upstairs.

But in the waxy darkness,
when I bite him, or tear his hair,
he calls out, 'again, again'.

Sea of Galilee

I could never sleep outside
and, what's more, in a crowd,
lying by an inland sea.

The raffia mat made patterns
on my face. Mosquitoes
whined at small infected wounds,

while we lay scratching
on the hollowed ground. And then someone
slipped out of their bag, and one by one

we unzipped, our bodies moving
through grey night to greyer water.
We were snakes shuddering

off our clothes, which were like skins,
and without our clothes
our bodies were like souls.

We were like fishermen wading in,
and so we were like saints. And then again
like fish. We were the catchers

and the caught. We might have been waves
but for our calm dance of swimming
and sudden touches of skin on skin.

John Clare's Shoes

She invites me in. There are no doors;
each frame's become a hole.
There's the sigh of a thin curtain,

but walls have ears.
All night my pubic bone aches.
The waters build in me like seas.

I hear bodies slither in a bag,
couples coming breast to breast,
the child's early dawning words.

I stroke the stacked doors,
wishing I could lift
each hard oak-panel, stop the gaps.

It's day in the museum, and I'm haunted
by the intimacies of night, as if the house
had a thousand mouths, which would talk, talk, talk.

And then I see the shoes
in their glass coffin, unlaced,
black leather sides sagging, heels downtrod.

Clare's shoes have battered tongues,
worn soles that tramped
through sunken lanes of seeding grass, vamping

out of doors with heavy locks,
away from rooms
which babbled like gods.

Echo

They say she's a late talker, haunting the garden,
digging mud-ovens to cook weeds.

Alone, sun lighting up closed curtains,
she'll jab her fingers into bowls of silver ash,
as if the glitter dust she dabs on hands and arms
will make her visible.

When there is a space in the air for the word to fit
among the jigsaw pieces of other people's speech,
when she feels the word's first stirring in her mouth,

aware of its shape, the breath it takes, then she starts
her tongue moving, saying it once, saying it once more,
and with every word, an echo.
                            Did she say it?
Did she hear herself say it?
                            She looks in mirrors
to see her own mouth move. She looks in mirrors
mouthing at herself, like Narcissus, the way
he loved his own reflection. And she's both
Narcissus and Echo, calling shun, shun,
reflect, shun, fleck, shun, reflection,
checking the mirror to see if she's still there
whispering each phrase again, loving, *loving*
to see her voice clothe itself in bones and skin, *skin*,
to see the whispers misting the glass,
and the shape on the surface where her lips pressed
showing, before it fades, a ripple, a *kiss*.

Water on the Moon

My father says, 'They've found water
on the moon.' Sheets and frozen depths of it.
We're going up.
The lift walls are as pitted as a cratered surface,
as shiny metallic as a child's silver-foil crescent,
pressed with creases.

They have found ice
                    hidden in the wells of the moon.
Galileo's dark seas are solid pools
                    clamped under the rocks of the moon.
They know what to do with moon-ice, how to mine it,
                    melt it into breath and fuel.
Visitors to the moon will return under their own steam.

When the doors open
we hear of water and blood hiding
in the kelpy spaces of my mother's lung.
There's an ebb and flow in her chest, a secret sea.

Returning late,
I see the moon, misty and waterlogged,
lighting my way past the night-closed crocus,
past the myrtle bush spiked by fierce peppery leaves,
and the myrtle is as dark and as mediterranean in the watered light
as my mother's eyes, growing larger
with every sigh of her secret sea.

Fireclay

First you strip to the waist,
then you pull off the lid,
dip in your hands.

I like the way you scoop
the clay on finger ends.
I like the thick whitecreaminess of clay.

I like your bare back and chest
that I have kissed and touched.
I cannot speak to you.

You step into the chimney.
You take the clay and start
to mould it on the brushed surface
of the bricks. You're eager
to patch the crack,
make another skin.

My dark man, with the pale skin,
soon you will be darkened by soot,
whitened by clay.

And later, out of the fireplace,
all your coolness will burn against me,
while the clay dries,
and the fire goes on escaping through the crack.

Don Giovanni's Puppeteer

What you don't see:
the pulling on of opaque black legs,
the long-sleeved leotard,
my coarse fair hair flattened with spray,
the black hood drawn skull-tight.

Luis advising me, his breath in my ear.

Mothballs, patchouli oil,
white dust in the velvet cloak,
the skin of all the actors
for the past hundred years.

I begin at the feet
sliding mine in, become his soles.
I fasten the anklets tight,
buckle our belts at the waist,
wear a loose canvas noose
about my neck, clip it neatly to his collar.
When I've slipped my hands in his,
Luis binds our wrists.

You choose not to see
how I've become his bones,
his dancing spine, a tree
of bloodbranches he can hang on,
how I can twitch his pelvis,
or jerk him down to hell.

And when you've gone
and he's untied us,
Luis loves him, talks to him,
retouches his papered face with paint,
mends the tiny gathered stitches in his breeches.

I strip, graze my knees
in the shallow littered pool,
hear the evening liners coming in,
watch tram lights ripple, magnify

blue tiles; I open and close
my own legs, letting the day-warmed water in,
thinking of what you don't dream, will never see,
Luis, this morning early,
saying he wants me standing,
turning my face to the wall,
lifting my arms from my side,
fumbling for my heart.

The Trip to Monterey

You drive over the river
the Mexicans wade nightly.

You're wearing a straw hat for protection,
shell earrings, a sea-coloured silk shirt.

You've lined your eyes with kohl
that you bought in Tunis,

made a picnic, white rolls, cheese,
bottled water. Bangles slide down your arm.

I'm guessing images that were true
in other places. Knowing what happened,

I've never asked what happened.
Instead I remember you leaving Walton Street,

the egg you refused to waste,
propping it between drawings,

driving it home, cross-country,
in the hired van. Your tenderness for things:

I remember you saying goodbye
to an antique infuser

dangling its perforated silver
back into its box. You hated

to break a plate, stain a cup.
And you'd been across oceans,

safely, waving your wild eastern hands.
I cannot imagine the road from Brownsville,

the old drunk careering in his car.
I cannot imagine the burning of you,

flesh and bone.
What I can see is the egg,

rolling from your mother's table,
the blood-spot quivering on the imagined floor.

The Wheedling Man

Just because he spoke in a wheedling sort of way,
just because he looked ashamed and afraid,
just because he whined and crouched,
just because he was so aware of his lost life,
fingering the old bus-pass in his pocket,
the photograph of his wife, just because
he drew his jacket round him against the cold
even though it was a warm blue day,
just because he puckered his face and looked like he might cry,
or suddenly piss on the venerable paving stones,
just because he wouldn't let up, was desperate
and sad, I didn't give him anything.
And now it's no consolation
to the hungry wheedling man, that he's stayed in my head
and won't go away, that I can replay every word of what he said,
how he looked; that I'm still walking down the lovely old alleyway
with its famous trace of an open sewer,

swishing my feet in gold-fingered horsechestnut leaves,
thinking of this man I meet everyday at four for sex,
(but not so crudely as that, in a kind of haze)
when he gets up from under the wall and approaches me,
his voice whining in my ear, his tweedy jacket
brushing my shoulder,
please love love please love spare me some change
dancing in front of me, stopping me getting on.
But two hours earlier, a man
with matted hair and Rasputin eyes
said to me firmly, 'I need two pounds, Give it me.'
And I gave instantly.

Mud Bath

Sitting down in the mud,
we pack it tight on skin,
delicately finger it under eyes,
massage it into breasts and inside thighs,
shape each other's backs,
as if sculpting mud onto a frame. Now we are
wild women, wild men, the first people of the early world,
made from earth and water to stare at the sky,
our feet growing from the ground.

When we stand, the gaps we leave,
fill like quicksand
as if we've taken nothing from the earth.

Our eyes peer through holes in mud-masks,
as we lean in the sun, statues drying,
the thick wet glaze turning to plaster.
Then we come alive, and, cracking as we move,
slide into sulphurous water,
let our feet drift, see our moulds
loosen, lift, dissolve,
grey clouds swirling in the hot spring.

We dry out on beach mats,
watch alligators, in the farm next door,
open jaws, slowly snap, sink into mud,
only their eyes visible through the barrier,
watching us, now we are flesh again.

Dialect

You say the children beat it out of you,
the Donegal rhythm, the immigrant words.

When you sing, your pitch is perfect,
but when you speak, you are untrue.

I like your tongue
in my mouth, or licking my nipple,
making what is soft, hard; your sharp wolf's teeth, I like them.

I think I know lies even when I suck them from you.

You tell how once, in Austria, you waded through snow
to pick the last bright apple from a black tree.

When I bite your skin,
your fictions are cidery on my tongue.

Where do voices go?

They're buried in your chest, your lungs,
return when you lie dying. They are here,
between my breasts.

I dream of you dying.

Your voice still tastes of bitter, of big-leafed tobacco burning smoke.
You still go down on me, in a wood, at night;

my hair is in the earth,
my back is damp with fallen beech.

You say it was a dream,
but it's amber, hardened by my body's memory.

This September

my nail splits hips
to find the spring:
dog roses,
packed tight as itchy seeds,
in skin,
red as the berry
in your lung,
which overgrew more wildly
than the hedgerow briar,
choking our footpath
to the field,
where now rooks gather,
breaking their reserve,
the near silence of summer.

Trevail (I)

You won't remember
how we fetched the mortice
from the farm, big as a castle-key
and how it wouldn't work at first
and how the cottage was forbidden.

You won't remember
the small cotton shirt
my mother gave you
and how I ran rainwater
into the stone sink of the spence,
washing the blue cotton in water so soft
the suds wouldn't rinse
but dripped on dry marram and plantain.

You won't remember the cornflowers
I bought in Nancledra,
easily slotting the money through
the slit of the black metal box.

You won't remember their ragged blueness
how they shone a blue light in the brown jug
as if we'd torn fragments out of the sky
and put pieces of air in the dark room.

You won't remember that I left you one evening,
climbed down through the lichen jungle,
ran down to River Cove on the river path
and watched seals, slick black commas
rolling in the waves, noses surfing,
surfacing on rocks.

You won't ever know or remember
the giddy pull of the seals basking
or the way I could have waded out
to meet them, nose to nose.

You won't remember my return
through the gate of the bouldered garden
or how I saw the blue shirt blowing,
dry and aired, tugging
at the hills of Wicca and Trevail.

You won't ever remember how
the small blue shape of your shirt
brought me back.

Three Definitions of Volume

We can find no scar,
But internal difference –
Where the Meanings, are – Emily Dickinson

A big white cracked rectangle, *sink*,
sopping ribbed sleeves and happiness –
that you could fit this into this into this
filling dented aluminium jugs with water
slopping one into the other or eight into one
gripping the black bakelite handles:
eighth (toy size), quarter pint,
a half-pint, a pint, quart, gallon
lining up the jugs like Russian dolls
teetering in order on the porcelain edge.
You might have been five, six, seven
less than half the mass you are now, and a sixth of your age
inside the same body. With one sip (from a wine glass, a cup, a mug,
the miracle of unchanging volume changing shape)
you replay

the word **vol** on a red plastic knob
and the hand that wouldn't or couldn't
turn it down and the throat that couldn't
stop screaming, the sound echoing all day

through *David Copperfield*, blue buckram with gold inlay,
faded copperplate inscription, pressed spider in the centre,
torn spine, mildewed paper which smells of sick,
through *Jane Eyre*, second hand,
fat octavo, red pasteboard, tiny print,
a woman in flames crying for water
which gushes from the tap while the jugs clink,
the children chatter and slide on the wet floor;
and you're wondering whether you really saw
the sun in the water and ladled it right up
into the gallon jug in a rippling skein
of shining cold reflection.

There is water; there are books; there is sound;
in French, vol = theft, vol = flight.
What could make you mad, makes you write.

In the Lane

We are speaking of the killing of children,
and I'm waiting for her to say,
'the world 's gone bad,'
wanting a comfortable reply,
wanting to see her with her sisters
in an old-fashioned pose, pinafore on,
feet slipping in the safe sunny lane
between the wars, *poor but happy*.
Instead, she says, 'Something I've never told…'
how walking back from school
in an untidy knot of children,
she'd raised her head
to an oak, the ivy twisting round the trunk,
the big tree shadowing and dappling
the lane's limestone walls. She'd raised
her head to laugh and seen the man
perched high. He had them in his sights.
She saw his finger tightening on the gun.
My seven year old mother
couldn't run or scream
or nudge the others, but stood
as if the coldest stillest girl on earth.
Someone shouted,
'A lorry's coming. Move!'
The children fell into the gateway of a field.
When she looked up, her pinafore was smeared
with mud and sand, a reason for her tears.

And through these last months,
I've pushed her home along the lane, thinking
how none of this might ever have happened.

Madron Well

Well: a source of water supposed to be of miraculous origin
or to have supernatural healing powers.

We've read about it so we follow
the unmarked path between hazels,
longing to get out of the close valley
to the saltiness of sea air.
'Is this it?' we ask, staring at mud.
But at the second pool,
the rustle of rags startles us:
slither of Liberty silk, a linen sleeve,
shredded silver foil, a chiffon scarf,
a school sock ringed with sweat,
bra straps, denim, unravelled wool, belts, ties.

What makes this holy is not the seep
of water in the muddy grass, but the vision
of a businessman running from the layby
where he's parked his Porsche,
slipping off his jacket,
tearing a sleeve from his shirt,
the school boy removing his sock, limping home
his left foot rubbing inside his trainer,
the young mother unhooking her bra
leaking milk into her cotton dress,
and the others who makes wishes for others
cutting string vests, old knickers,
handkerchiefs with stitched initials,
the stretching up of their tensed bodies,
their fingers knotting relics to the hazel,
praying that no one sees them do it,
then praying for a cure.

Sometimes you give me your old clothes:
I wish I was wearing your Indian skirt
and could do what you would hate,
rip it into blue and white strips,
tie them above the water,
the source of some pagan healing
of which you wouldn't approve.

Aliens

In the summer that my granny's mouth went strange,
her tongue sideways, frustrating her lips,
her words a scrawl of pencil on a pad,
my mother was always driving,
taut as a string pulled between two posts,
her hands sharp on the sandwich bread,
slapping thick doorsteps onto formica,
reversing in at midnight,
and up early in a clatter of angry pans.
One night when it was morning already,
she'd sat thinking of her mother's life,
her hand held tight watching her,
and then driven back in a low gear,
winding through the village where she was born
and up high through trees, tired
by her imaginings of an empty bed
with clean white sheets.
As her car climbed dark boughed bends,
lighting garlic, startling deer,
and the valley fell away beneath,
the sky grew larger, and she saw
a ring of faces in the air
looking down at the hill, the beeches,
looking down at her.

My father talked of night manoeuvres,
but my mother shook her head,
not helicopters, not planes, but faces
that formed a face she never saw again.

Birth

A story children love to hear
but can never remember.
'She was born on'…
a biographer's note
that says nothing
of the day in December
your sixteen year old mother
and your father
struggle with the cold,
stopping gaps in the plaster
with his granny's torn petticoat,
laying scarves and old socks
against the undercracks of doors,
lighting the gas which seeps
into running flames along each wall.
When you come slithering out,
they name you Myrtle
for the cottage which leaks fire and rain
while your mother sluices
herself down with water from the china jug
and your father fills his pipe
and worries and coughs
thinking how he really is a man
now he has a child. And you can't remember
any of it: Old Daise, your mother's stepmother,
embarrassing your mother
with a Romany blessing
and some eggs from the goose.

Before the six other children,
before the sixty-a-day Senior Service,
before the horses,
there is just you and them, and, after the rain,
winter sun whitens the old man's beard
which loops from beech to yew to beech
tracing the whole steep hill, and there is
your mother, bloody, and singing
with her long hair down,
the way you always wanted to remember.

Walking to Stedham Mill

Trying to sense a ghost,
you startle a naked woman
by Iping church. She stands
still in the quiet heat
looking out
across the field
you're looking out across.

After stagnant stretches
of garlic, wilting bluebells
pour themselves through woods.
The old road leans
over the water.

At the mill house,
the generator's unused.
The stepping stones,
rivered by weed,
are unused. Dizzy, you grip
the metal rail firmed
into the slabbed concrete bridge
and stare down
at the weir of glass,
green–brown bottle glass,
turning white,
all ozone and spray.

Screaming boys
leap from the sluice,
bum-first into the mill pool,
gasping in the woody water,
crashing through the current
to the deep nettled bank.

You walk on
to Woolbeding
through stitchwort, soapwort,
archangel and vervain,
walk home on the high path
breathing yellow rape,
hearing a boy's voice
float downriver.

Reflux: the Japanese Bridge at Giverny

For years you quell water-weeds,
struggle with the sun,
strive for clouds in your water-trap,

letting the fall of water, the floating Os
catch light and wind between their gaps.
But the clouds you've watched seep in,

fogging agapanthus, irises.
You walk the garden
in a mist. You can see Blanche,

sedulous, picking caterpillars
from each nasturtium leaf, knowing
they'll be stripped,

the orange faces shredded.
The wisteria's a crude tangle of ropes.
The lilies are smeared white-gold.

You shout, 'I call this yellow.
What do you call it?'
Amnesia of colour.

You're forced to squint,
reading *sienna* (intermittent
bleeding) *red*,

cobalt (drowning)
blue, painting by word
in a torture of monochrome.

And after the knife,
the waiting,
head sandbagged,

no sudden moves,
month after month of black flecks
in your sights, until

the new glasses from Germany,
and the bridge suddenly burning
trees and earth together,

a hell on water,
raging in ochre, in orange,
demanding you.

The Return

A heron has left
prints in the clay
under clear slow water.

I put my hands through clouds
and swirl the sky away
until the water becomes
its own earthy cloud.

My fingers are prying for a life
I've never found here
though I've heard my father
remember sticklebacks, eels,
the day the poisoned slurry
filled the ditches

and then nothing for thirty years
but water
and the storm-branches
we used to gather
trying to dam the stream.

On damp shale islands,
I find movement
on the underside of stones,
the busy sidling of freshwater shrimps,
and, in the rain-washed rubble
of lime, chalk, flint,
among the smooth trickling fragments
of brick, there's a flicker,
a quick comma curve,
the stoneshaded bullhead
escaping the sun
nudging his blunt face
to a rock.

My children are making dams
but the water eludes them,
spilling into the hook of the bend
under the trunk of fallen beech
they'll shin across
to the wild side.

Trevail (II)

Hands on the iron gate,
moving its shadow
cast on grass,

I touch safety and hear
the voices of the men
sailing Wicca pool

their words floating up,
until gentled by their tones,
warm as the heather

on the narrow safe
walk home, I duck
under the whale's rib

to the garden grown
wild with fuchsia: not
perfect, not elegant

drops, not bloody drops,
but open mouths, showing
purple tongues, imperial as murex,

or underskirts revealing
the tender inside,
the stamens long and gold,

dusty threads
growing pollen
to draw the bees.

JENNY LEWIS

My Face

is changing again
I caught it in a different light
yesterday

the flaky grey
of ocean-going
tankers

my face has turned
to someone else's

inside the inside
of the ocean, fish are hanging
cuttle-coloured

they sway, silent
not even a rattle of bones

and the dead stir in us too,
coming as they do from the weight
of darkness

they want our breath

want to tunnel out of us,
force apart our gullets,
appear stark-white

and raving at daylight

one more moment
they plead
just one more

Five Billion Years of Secrets

Summer comes, soft-footed to the doorway,
slips over the sill, threadless and shining;
filling us again with the old yearning,
making us want to skip work for the day.

High in the Altai, Umai shakes her grey,
tattooed leather free from ice and, turning
in her grave, gives off a smell of burning;
Kali is also on the move, they say.

Meanwhile, on Jupiter, the mean wind speed
is three hundred and thirty miles an hour –
a storm the size of Earth which shows up red

on NASA's screens. And far from Ganymede,
Callisto, most similar to our own
life-giving planet, is (already) dead.

Aubade

She thinks of bread and butter, sliced thin;
a brown egg, smooth as a knuckle;
a cup of milk, slightly warmed,
already forming a brave new skin.

Then later, chocolates, sweet wine,
maraschino cherries, shiny in syrup,
reflecting squares of brash light; cream
whipped to an adolescent frenzy.

But lying here with him, the budding light
is so far painless. She waits for him to wake
with appetite refreshed by sleep – knowing
that what he enjoys most is her hunger.

Prospects

We lay, a dormitory of ten year olds, deciding
which death would be preferable – our summer skins
watermarked by smears from mushy flannels now
stiffening on washroom pipes to pungent, dried, marine
shapes. With hands that smelt of pencil shavings we proved
self-strangulation was impossible, although our
gluey fruit-gum mouths ran technicolour trying it

Burning from the feet up like Saint Joan would be worst,
someone suggested. *You'd faint before it got too bad –*
the sturdy girl cut out to be a nurse assured us.
But until then? Remembering the courage test
of fingers over candle flames, we shared the pop
and prick of sizzling flesh, the smell of singeing hair,
and slowly drew our knees up, hugged ourselves.

Yet drowning would be just as horrible, we knew
from when we held our breaths in swimming; a gallery
of underwater fossil shapes in black wool costumes,
buoyant on our silver strings of seed pearl bubbles,
while springboard plunges boomed and banged; swerves
of light made wavy lines along the tiled bottom,
our lungs cracked, and our eyes bulged like onions.

How many of us are left? How many count the days
to humdrum endings, seeing death now as a release
from tyrannies we couldn't know about as children;
loneliness that comes at night in strangling ropes,
fear and hopelessness settling like moths over the heart;
and the knowledge that we're fated by our wombs and breasts
to be buried, screaming, with the old, dead king.

Slag

i.

Growing up in its shadow,
seems its gritty dust
wants to get into her knickers,
soils the armholes of her vests
even before she sprouts hair there.

Her mam looks away,
keeps on polishing –
the slap of her duster a reproach
to her daughter, to the men.

She's sixteen now and their lamp eyes
follow her. She's outgrown
her school photo, bakes
better than teacher, is fond
of walks and puppies, knows nothing
of wrecked bronchia, shafted lives.

ii.

Summer evenings, coming up
through lakes of vetch and loosestrife,
air moist as cow's breath, smelling of
cud and fodder; and her breasts swing
slow as an udder, making the boys gasp
and the girls run ahead to shouting distance.

Their dads were right;
she gives to the first who asks,
buries her face in the slack of their shirts,
never hears the tip begin to slide.

iii.

Her mam cries into a spotless hanky,
wipes the muck from her daughter 's face,
thinks how peaceful she is, how lucky.

At the funeral they wear beads of jet
as is the tradition in the valleys,
coal black and hard as a set jaw –
a mark of respect for those who died.

Bright Morning

for Tom

Coming into the bright morning as he used to,
quietly, feeling his way round the edges of silences,
appearing suddenly in doorways, smiling,

he witnessed scenes Vermeer could have painted –
a child stripping redcurrants, a woman with a letter,
a cat cleaning its paw, a man drinking from a pint pot.

Now he says he watched it all as if from a distance,
like looking through a fishbowl at potbellied colours
and shapes bleeding sideways – the child at the window,

the woman crying, the man turning away; and inside
him, none of the brightness he brought to them,
but only despair and coldness, like a moonstone

where his heart should have been. He preferred
the garden, looking over the valley with its boundless
moments; its possibilities lying thick as grass stems

for him to chew over. His dens had entrances
only a small child could get through, and there he hid –
behind the old milking parlour, under the laurel,

between the holly hedges, in the drapes of the willow.
Is that where he transports himself to now – away from
the grey and black of Manchester, the concrete stairwells,

the bad trips, the broken, the dying, the empty cans,
the kicked dogs? Or is it possible he feels
this life's at least more honest than those childhood

tableaux. And if he could look again, would he trample
down the barriers, and stampede through to this bright morning
where the paintings have, at last, been turned to the wall?

Woman Brushing Her Hair

after Degas

In spring, I lived underwater with it –
my mackerel hands held auburn hanks
like uncoiled ropes to brush and brush,
while my thoughts drifted upwards
into the pearly green and umber.

By summer, my face was a scribble –
no eyes, a mute mouth. I forced the auburn
from its lair at the nape of my neck,
brushed it over my brow in torrents
with hands like ham bones. By now
I knew I couldn't tame it by myself.

That autumn, I sat on a bed while my maid
tried to groom it. 'Does it hurt?' she asked,
as the auburn itself fell like a curtain
over any other possibilities my life held.
She tilted her head and pulled, spilling
a ginger snakeskin over my face and forearms.

In winter, roasting chestnuts, I was caught
in the blaze. My dress became flames.
My maid grabbed the inferno and tried
to brush it out. A jigsaw of shapes held us firmly
in place while in one corner, just in the picture,
a dab of pearly mackerel.

Lupins

with their peppery, summery smell,
filled the moment to its joyous rim,
lifting the shadow my father left by dying.

Eight years of living with my mother's grief
wiped clean by the heat and promise of the day.
And I, a small child, tending my garden,

shedding the past for that moment's clarity;
absorbed and delighted by the task's simplicity,
planting stones in a rough circle; turning up worms

the colour of corsets, hardly aware that time
was passing; of the smell of gym shoes
and grass being cut, or the way the heavy

summer air curved the sound
of four o'clock striking.

Now, lupins always remind me of you.
Your slow, smiling energy, your quiet sureness –
lifting the stain of childish sorrows,

keeping the day bright like a sun-warmed
garden; until night comes and our spirits venture –
silently, hand in hand, without fathers;

black as lupins at dusk,
setting out against a tall sky.

Balcony

The daffodils had sooty trumpets
like herald angels from the poorer part
of heaven. Our granny planted them

with bulbous winter fingers
around Christmas. She told us stories
about Lazarus and Nazarenes

and Gaderene swine falling from the cliffs.
She said *hark*! instead of *listen*!
and – *you can't make a silk purse*

out of a sow's ear. No, I said
it would be cruel to the sow.
She didn't hear.

Hark! Hark! the Lark! sat open
on the old German piano with its
scuffed legs and treacly varnish.

Your Tiny Hand is Frozen
on the wind-up gramophone
sounded like an asthma attack

until it got going. Sometimes I hid
behind the daffodils to catch sounds
as they came up. A girl my age

down the road sat at her window
like a smudge in a painting book.
Her mother fell down once with bags

full of empties like jingle bells.
Another time some boys came round
the corner shouting –

Christ I need a fuck! My balls
ache! My granny was sleeping.
I put on *Jerusalem the Golden*.

Getting On

It seems as if, overnight, the position has changed.
There's another generation coming up from London
for the weekend, full of noisy gossip about the latest
Festival Hall ingenue, the tiresomeness of tube trains
and what Harold Pinter has been getting up to lately.

Where once it was our children who rampaged down
farm tracks in their Cloth Kits and Fairisle, now it is
the Osh Kosh and Benetton babies, hell bent on making
their parents' lives a misery, who tack and squall along
the hedgerows in red, Paddington Bear wellies. While we

surprise ourselves – accept the consolation of quieter
pleasures, like having our own study and always writing
with a good pen. And as the lunchtime sherry and the
ladies' flower rota begin to sing a faintly
siren song, the thatched cottage by the Post Office

far too small for the up and coming family, now
twinkles a shy welcome that is not entirely sniffed at.
And even the elderly husband, once the butt
of wine bar jokes by girls in mini-skirts of mock-velour,
is seen in a more kindly light as he comes, in slippers,

bearing shaking mugs of cocoa – always fine bone china
decorated by the National Trust with wayside flowers
or garden birds – to remonstrate, as the church clock creaks
eleven, saying 'Here we are my dear, time to put
down your poetry and come to bed. It's getting on.'

Seal

Cowl of water
round a whiskery face,
an old nun basking
in remnants of sunshine.

Flippers clasped like hands praying,
she blows out roundly
through serene nostrils,

hearing the surf's
answering vespers;
sucked breath of shingle,
cascade
of pebbled rosaries.

Light stains the sea
to windows
of red and gold

as texture of salt air
coarsens. Cloistered waves
slap rocky sacristies.

Shutting her nostrils to slits
seal dives, sensing, perhaps,
the tug of fatal currents

something cold beached
somewhere

and the night air,
chill as confessions
in an empty church.

Dear Field

don't let me talk to you as if you were a woman,
that's an easy cliché – your mounds and dips,
your tufts by gurgling hollows – but dear field,
you are more than this; patiently taking the mud-squelch

of cattle, ricochet of may bugs, bees buzzing
in a cupped hand of clover. Beneath bent blades,
light dips unwinking as a cockerel's eye;
chaotic flecks; a cage of shade which hoops

and casks kaleidoscopes of beetles. While I pilot
my shape between computer and tea kettle – a brief
image going bent quick as a flicker book before

flickering out – you remain. Your small hill sporting
its spindly mohican still head-butts the sky each spring –
always will. For my daughter. For my daughter's daughter.

Poems for Peter 1:

Last Visit

The letter box opened like a slit pod,
and your voice, whispering on air-mail,
sounded thin, papery, starved of jokes.

The Spanish idyll, you said, was over;
one tumble too many over the edge
in your off-road vehicle;

black dog, hair-of-the-dog
and hair-pin bends finally got you.

Back in Belsize Park,
it wasn't you I visited, but some
fractious infant in an old man's body,

huddled by the gas fire. The gargling
noise was you, trying to say something.
Eventually I made it out.

You were telling Maureen
to send me away.

Poems for Peter 2:

Losing Your Voice

You started to lose your voice in Spain;
didn't need it when light slipped, lizard-like
into a basking heap at the base of walls.

The stripped cork trees round your house
had tabby patterns, like your cats,
melting into plaits of mauve and olive, like
something vaguely thought of but not yet spoken.

In the mid-distance, bulls stood, monumental,
waiting their turn in the ring at Ronda.

On a clear day, if they knew it, they could see
Morocco, or past the ragged emptiness
to Granada's high sierras.

We avoided views
in the late-afternoon when the plants
in your finca leaned against the heat;

an intense quiet broken only by goat bells
and cicadas. At dusk, in the Bar Espana,
you didn't need words for Juan or Cristobal

to set up your usual – *cerveza* then *vino*,
slugs of rough brandy. You said nothing,
just swerved on your way to Bar Flores

which made the locals hail you wildly
with shouts of *hombre malo!* You responded
with your clenched-fist salute; and, coming home
there was a violent moon.

Stags strode into our lights.
A wild boar shook its tusks,
then disappeared.

The twisting path was ready
to throw us off at every bend. If only you
had gone then – grabbed in a flash
by the Spanish night.

Poems for Peter 3:

Maureen's Story

Walking up Haverstock Hill at 3 a.m., there's no traffic,
no one. Sounds deadened by flakes falling thick and quiet.
The kerb bandaged with white, only your own footsteps
making tracks. It couldn't happen so suddenly, could it?

The phone call waking you, a voice, disembodied, young,
telling you you needn't come now if you didn't want to.
Then getting dressed, alone, walking alone up Haverstock
Hill. The snow falling and everything white; so different

from normal it's like a dream. Nothing prepares you
for this, you think. (As if you wouldn't want to come!)
Everything gowned in white, unreal and empty
as a hospital corridor. No need to hurry, you're

already too late. There's no fear, no tiredness, nothing;
just the strangeness of being out on your own in the dark,
before the milk float. All the dazzle and din of your lives
tucked in and folded under by this sheet of snow.

Walking up Haverstock Hill at 3 a.m., reaching the hospital,
finding the ward empty except for him on the bed,
everything disposed of, his effects shoved into black bags.
They give you coffee in a plastic cup. He's still warm

when you kiss him but there's no Peter any more,
and only the journey home, carrying bin bags, your tracks
covered almost before you make them. Walking back
down Haverstock Hill, blinking away the snowy light.

Anchoress 3: Unio Mystica

At first I seemed to be drowning; my self
diffusing out and down into unsearchable
deepness. As if a sound, a million points,
scintillas of high notes like a robin's song
crushed into particles, was dissolving –
a dissolution of all in me that is
dissolute, unsaved, unsavable;
like coloured motes of a church wall-painting,
drifting on the choir's breath, or tapestry
stitches, freed from warp and weft, floating
suddenly meaningless without frame.

Then I realised I was melting, liquified,
streaming golden as honey, the fire
outside and in me, the sight of it
outwardly blinding yet making blindness
a way of seeing; the heat unbearable
and welcome, white as an orchard at Easter,
the love-pain unspeakable yet longed for,
packed in surprising sweetness like my cold
finger testing jam at boiling point,
or poking coals in the coned bread oven
while waiting for the third day rising.

At last I knew the melting was red blood
like my own, yet a dearer, sacred blood.
My senses were birds, nesting in his five
wounds. Site of peace, city of Zion, my
eyes become doves meekly to approach you.
When I myself am the city, I am filled
with music which is the food of heaven.
I am a garden of scents. When my bridegroom
comes, I am a flower opening in his heart.
We are one – he is courteous and homely.
Then, now and ever, all is well.

Acknowledgements to Richard Rolle, Jane Draycott,
Lesley Saunders, Helen Farish.

Watching the Eclipse from Brill Hill

We looked through cellophane of triple
thickness, mauve and red; and suddenly
clouds shifted and the sun blazed crescent,
Arabic, a metal brazier

spilling a weird light; and people sky
watching, faces turned like satellite dishes
to the black disc, saw it circled by
a diamond ring, like something from

the Argos catalogue; children raced
up hill, as if an ending wasn't
imminent. A baby slept in its pram
its face brass-coloured, and a spaniel,

barking wildly, breasted breakers
of grass. Brill windmill, medieval, stood
stubbed into the ground beneath the hill's
crest, as if daunted by the dawn of a time

in which antiquity stood for nothing.
We unwrapped our picnic – an apple
a bun, three rice cakes and a camembert
sandwich, washed down with plastic thermos

coffee. We thought the encircling movement
of the moon across the sun was like
a man and woman embracing. It seemed
as if the moon, the female, moved across

and then moved on, freeing herself from arms
that could no longer hold on to her. It was
as if she took the ring and hurled it far
away across the strangely coloured valley.

Last Rites

Last night I laid some flowers at a grave,
daffodils, thick-stemmed, leaking sap and milk,
and letters in a box of cedarwood,
five mornings on a Spanish hillside, with vines
well-hung, a fruitful rosary: a photo
of that boat trip when the grey swell hurled us
high against the curling walls of water.
Seals slunk from rocks, slid from slabs, and a few
last shags, heraldic on limestone henges,
spread wings to dry like gutted black umbrellas.

We saw our wake make glassy coils that snaked
away, like you, as slippery as silk.
Last night I laid some flowers at our grave:
daffodils, thick-stemmed, leaking sap and milk.

Martin's Car

It is a throne, pale blue; and when
she is in it, she plays the queen,
hair streaming out in a tangled crown.

It stands low to the ground on a cloak
of purple shadow. Inside, the seats
are soft as ermine. He kneels in reverence

to wipe its hub caps. She, impatient for power,
commands him to use his key,
set the thing throbbing. The cloak turns

ragged, flies out over the roads
like coronation flags. The roar is crowds
at their accession. They come

to a cornfield, stop at the verge,
process through bowing stalks,
woven with waving poppies' heraldry.

She is gracious, allows him favours, grants
him liberties. He lies at her feet and swears that
he will be her subject – if she will be his object.

Book Lovers

Let's meet tonight between the covers
to thumb each other's spines
like true book lovers.

Steamy passion or sweet romance,
with titles picked at random,
our mood will depend on chance.

I'll stroke your hard back and thighs,
trail my fingers over your fly-
leaf – admire your point size.

You'll enjoy ogling my index,
fondling my frontispiece, thinking
I'm just the type you like for sex.

I'll let you flip my pages, skim
my contents, skip my appendix
or linger over my fine lines at whim.

And if I get pregnant (which I won't)
let's meet again – in nine months time.
You choose the font.

JOE SHEERIN

Alter Id

Growing wary of everyone my suspicions
Finally came to rest on myself.

At night I study my face in the mirror
For tell-tale signs of deceit

Blood on the gums a sure augury
Of a heart on the threshold of breaking

A tired or sloping tongue can only mean
The kiss of life administered or received

Moist lips are a presage of hope. The groom
Leading the bride to the parting gate.

My cunning eyes avoiding my own gaze
Show a guilty conscience an urge to run.

I check for pink smudges on the bridge of the nose
An au-revoir planted in a doorway on tiptoe.

Phone numbers on newspaper margins or small
Talismans are signs that things are not what they seem.

Finally I go through the pockets for double
Bus tickets, theatre stubs, motel match books.

I find dust and small change only. There is nothing yet
To turn suspicion to fact. But I need watching.

Beatitudes

Having everything except love
and money I count my blessings
on the fingers of both hands.

First there are the trees that kiss
cheeks and shake their flounced petticoats.
I bend one little finger to the palm.

For the fliers that unzip the slinks of night
and the bullfinch that dresses up the morning;
two more fingers make half a fist.

Another one is the sight of horses streaming,
the index, the trigger happy, the bachelor, the wind
finder, the Don Juan, the explorer, the reader in the dark.

The luxury of green silence. I count this
on the stubby thumb, the pipe's tamp
the bell push, the inside nipple, the counter of notes.

One fist made, I lower my sights
to the left hand the sinister side. I count
now the misfortunes of my neighbour.

Abbey

After one thousand years the Abbey
is returning itself to the hills, a stalagmite
of shaped stone melting back into the earth.

The trees are knocking in the open door
of the chapel and the grass is walking up the aisle
to the high altar. One sapling a camouflaged intruder
has perched itself impossibly on a shelf
of wall thirty feet up surveying the change.

In the silence of the evening we are
the only worshippers. It is easy at this pious hour
to recall the centuries of celebration,
matins and lauds and vespers day after day.
Even the stones should have learned worship.

This is a little like love giving and turning
back into itself and returning to the place it came from
undiminished but different and always needing
to start again fresh dug from the ruins.

And you a fresh novice might come
breathtaking out of the broken but still holy
chapel apologizing for being late as usual.

Like Demosthenes I take a pebble on my tongue.
It sings in my mouth. My heart stammers.

Lovebirds

The common sparrow or a starling
first brought a cluster of faces to
the kitchen window. A thrush stopped
a heartbeat. A robin, always new,
made us long for his curious return.

Wishing like lovers for lovers' company
we joined societies, bought books and powerful
telescopes, became the peeping Toms
of woodpeckers and jays and nesting owls.

We lay in the grass all day to court
a pipit or tiptoed home at dawn from
strange woods where nightjars
rode the darkness on their specked wings.

A faint hope sent us breathless by car
or train, O love us, O love us, we called
to a Siberian crane out in the mud flats.
Marry me, marry me harlequin, we
pleaded into the vagrant wind.

We kept diaries as full of secrets
as schoolgirls, recording trysts that promised
so much and ended in a sigh of wings leaving.

That was last year's passion, now as stale
as old bread. We have tired of one-way love.
To-day I wouldn't cross the road for a phoenix.

Pleasure Seekers

There are some who love old buildings; cathedrals
Are a favourite, the long aisled walk from the salt font
To the high altar and the broken heart of stained glass.

Underfoot the flat memory of dead merchants' families,
Old men, buxom wives and Tom Thumb children, now rest
Where placenta becomes clay and tongues no longer
Wag in the tight ground. Their very taste is in the air.

About the walls, Bishops and Knights incorruptible as
Alloy rest on their elbows and ladies with the rise
Of perfect breasts recline under the decency of bronze.

The recent dead stick to the walls like burrs, the dates
Of their departure too close for comfort while the candelabra
With its lisping light invites a penny for our thoughts.

Others have enough of death and its maudlin glory
And walk past into the bright day. Their pleasure

Only the sudden shock of tenanted beach, the holy
Salt of lips, the perfect dune of an arse.

Genesis

Make more cats said Mrs God
Not toads rats spiders snakes.
Make more swans not vultures
Hawks buzzards eagles kites.
But come in for your tea first.

At the bottom of Eden in a potting shed
He quickly kneaded a clay cat and swan
Blew on them and shut the door tight.

They ate ambrosia and honey from gold
Plates. Afterwards he helped with the washing up.

Finding a white neck speckled with blood
And a cat badly winged and given up
For dead she asked, Is this your idea

Of a joke? He went quiet and distant
The way gods do and wondered if they
Would ever make a go of it, she
Being such a perfectionist.

Local Historian

The chronicler of the street is at last as blind
as Homer. Falls of opaque water now
curtain her eyes. Once her sight could
pierce walls at night, x-ray souls through overcoats.

She watched it all, an Eve with an apple
in her apron pocket and a workman kneeling
to bite it. She handing his temples.

She saw Helen stolen while a husband
worked away. Wearing high heeled shoes and
bending to put her two suitcases in the boot
of his car. For a moment she understood why.

She saw a man who was born to duty and should
know better abdicate leaving his well-tended
kingdom and subjects for someone else. And exile.

She watched the war to end all wars fought
over thirty years ending in a long hearse and tears.

She watched a man's Waterloo of emphysema
A soldier shrunk now to a fist, bent double
grasping for air. His meek wife now becomes
a general, with polished gaiters and gold
epaulettes and a staff car at her disposal.

At night she heard the drone of bombs that
fell at random scattering families to smithereens.
Like the rest she hid in a cupboard holding
her head. In the morning or the following day
or maybe a week after she noted the carnage.

She watched the priest baptizing with one hand
and closing the eyelids of the dead with the other
and a lover kissing one set of lips and fondling another.
And two struggling up the frosty pavement
loaded with shopping and secrets some only
to be wrapped and opened while others remained
forever hidden behind the walls of the heart.
And children some laughing and some screaming
their voices merging until it was impossible to tell.

Now she sits and all day hears from outside
the harsh bite of apple, the slow moan of traffic.

Incident at a Post Office Counter

I weighed the package for Dublin.
The teller scratched his memory.
'Dublin? Is that Northern or Southern?'

I reassured him. He pushed the stamps
With his palm towards me like a croupier.

Licking them I couldn't help wondering
If his weakness was Geography or History.

Naming

Pity the mule the unloved beast of the badlands
Breaking the day's fast on whins and thistles.

The product of the horse's lack of judgement
And the ass's snobbery and an open gate.

Neither fish nor flesh a stubborn loner
With a cock like a cudgel that can breed no children.

Inside the farm-keep young of all kinds thumb their
Noses. No solace either in the litany of plants

Around him. Dogrose, catnip, cowparsley, horseradish.
His soft heart trembles at the almost of mulberry.

Because They Looked Down on Walkers

I learned to ride a bicycle but not
Being city born and more at home with mules
And cart horses, the fickleness of two
Wheels carried my country weight uneasily

So late an expert my tormentors
Too polite to spit looked scornfully
At me from their car windows as they passed.

Envy is a hard tutor. I took to the car
Like a hare to captivity, my wild eyes and nodding
Ears telling me too much for my own good.
There was no going back. By the time I learned
To park successfully I was a driver of sorts.

Always one jump ahead, my rivals now ride
Above me on hang-gliders or in planes, their faces
In the clouds, impossible to guess what
They are thinking if anything at all.

Too far gone to catch them, now I travel the by-roads
And watch for the two-wheeled or the drivers
Of asses, a heavy gob balanced on my tongue.

Elves

Take nine gifted elves, a bit of cosmic
jiggerypokery and a womb to work in.

The first is an eye maker because that's how
it all starts. He takes inspiration from magazines.

The second fashions the lips pouting
into a mirror until he gets it just right.

The third is a neck elf, unnecked himself
he works from imagination and Japanese prints.

The fourth will make the breasts having watched
drops in slow motion fall into a basin of water.

The fifth oversees the area between milk and honey
laying down a flat surface with room for expansion.

The sixth is as private as an undertaker, folding
and tucking charged nerves deftly under membrane.

The seventh is an aromatherapist blending from
juniper and privet and mandrake and coral and radish.

The eighth is a leglover. Finding feet pedestrian
he recalls soft-focus porn viewed from escalators.

The ninth designs the back. No great lover of Ingres
he plants knuckles of vertebrae, blades of shoulder.

All nine leave contented, not caring that in the course
of nine human months things may change for the worse.

Palmer's Kiss

Unsure of the future we visited
a fortune teller (we have a house,
enough money and two children
at a private school). But still we wanted
to be sure our luck would hold.

She held court in a small kiosk
on the pier of a seaside town. It
was cold autumn and we breezed in
fresh in furs, the eyes on some still moist.

She hardly looked up from behind
her counter. A headscarf enveloped her
hair and a cat raised one ear at our greeting.

Unused to protocol (we knew how to
behave at dinner parties, funerals,
post-graduate dos and weddings. But with a fortune teller?) – we knelt

Gold dangled from her ears
pearls shone in her eyes, rubies clung to her lips.

She took my right hand in hers, and with
one delicate finger slowly traced the lines
Oh, the joy.

Miracle

On the last night of the wake sitting alone
with the corpse and the candle and the stopped clock

The wind shooing the light across the ceiling
and lapping the faces of the new dead in shadow.

The room is as quiet as mice and downstairs
the old watch sleeps in the hold of the house.

Outside the June night is thick with conspiracies
of life under and on the ground and in the darting air.

You lie undisturbed your hair sleeked back and
your skin unworried by the tremor of a vagrant nerve.

Love is too weak to wish any bit of the past undone
and when they wet their eyes and say you died too young

I know the past was best and love's deceit waits ahead
and I would turn Jesus, fresh from the triumph of Lazarus,
away from your bed.

When It Happens

When it happens how will you kill
Your children? You could, being loving,
Cuddle them to death planting big smackeroos
On their dead ears.

Or you could, being medical, overdose them
On chocolate drink, spooning the last dross
Like medicine down their juddering necks.

Or you could, being dramatic, shoot them
Cleanly through the forehead, deliberately
Missing the apple placed playfully on their heads.

Or you could, being military, put them against
A wall and shoot them after some stirring music
And a court martial where the evidence was never in doubt.

Or you could, being religious, crucify them
And then, full of remorse, take them down and rub
Oil of aloe into the crevices of their palms.

Or you could, being cowardly, stab them
In the back when they are looking out a window,
Then run into a darkened room and hide.

Being childless you have no excuse for inaction.
The orphanages are brimming. Go and kill them
In the old way dispassionately.

Stalag

Last week from the closeness of our guarded
street a prisoner made a break for freedom.

She left in broad daylight without money or false
papers, disguised only in her best coat with lips
flared and rouge smeared in the hollows of her cheeks.

So audacious it took us all by surprise. We expected
flight by dust cart or dressed as a padre or a red
cross worker or the familiar uniform of the watch.

At night when the stars burned at infinity
beyond the lampposts and the breeze breasted the curtains
we wondered where her body filled the hollow of some bed.

Of course she was caught and led back handcuffed
to her children, the door closed and the curtains shut.

She went before the Kommandant. What happened
is unclear but there were shouts and whimpering and a loss
of face. Later she emerged wearing dark glasses and
a roll neck the kind we once used to hide love bites.

Closing Time

When the admirers have gone home
I feed the gibbon and the lion
Fruit and flesh bought at the corner shop.

The rhinoceros needs hay and the camel
Lips water prudently. The zebra
And the Polish horse relish the same mouthful.

The tiger feasts on the lamb and the puma
Licks blood from the armpit of the rabbit.

The antelope buries its snout in clover
And the caribou nibbles the pastures of dandelion.

I feed the crocodile on the softness of duck
And the piranha on the necks of swans.

Snakes open their hinged mouths for haunch of ox
And the angel-fish gulp the embalmed bodies of flies.

The bees are self-sufficient; the ants trim leaves
And wasps make paper for tomorrow's news.

Don't Ask

The bricklayer doesn't ask the brick
If it's comfortable there. If it lies snugly
Enough along the line and takes
The weight above it, it will do.

The roofer doesn't ask the tile if
It minds the weather. Cunning as survival
It casts the drop on the one below
Spreading the misery. The ground
Bulky and enough of it absorbs all.

The finished house doesn't ask the occupier
Who pays the bills or starts the arguments
Or whose turn it is to turn off the light.
It has learned its lesson and sits tight.

The spermatozoa doesn't ask the ovum who
Started the foreplay but gets down
To the business of geometric progression.
The finished baby lies like love on the carpet.

Ceremonies

I hate preliminaries
Grace before meals, lipping
the wine and smelling the cork

Kissing before love
making, small talk before kissing,
pregnancy before childbirth,
childhood before the real thing.

Arguing before the big bust-up
manoeuvres before the shooting war.

I hate the bit players before
the main actor, the failed comedian
before the funny man, the chorus
girls before the stripper, the clown
before the high wire walker,
the triple jump before the high wall,
the ball boys before the players
the umpire before the bowler
and the damned music before everything.

Most of all I hate long drawn out
illness, praying and drugtaking,
mending and regressing, ingrown
tears and fake jollity

when one could simply drop
dead in the middle of something.

Diaries

Tonight I read my first son's
childhood out. A sneak preview

I gather up his toys in armfuls
and put his books
of frog princes and wild geese and
pumpkin brides and dwarfs where they belong

He has crossed the rapid flood
into the sparse terrain where I range

Chest deep in muddy water holding
his innocence aloft like a gun, I draw
my breath in half hoping he will drown

He shakes himself like a dog on my ground
And now neither of us can go back.

The Last Days of Jesus

It's hard, knowing what's going to happen,
To make any plans. He neglected the garden,
Saw the lawn creep on to the drive and let
The two pointed conifers wither in their tubs.

He knew he should be out healing the sick
Or knocking on doors preaching the word,
Or casting out devils, or feeding the poor.

He didn't go for drinks after work. A spoilsport,
They called him. Nor did he weave a part in the light
Fabric of conversation or plan the next year's outing.

The few evenings left to him he would stand
At the back gate smoking looking over the fields
And watched the horizon darken before the falling sun
And the oaks spreading their arms in welcome.

SUE HUBBARD

Nude in Bathtub

after Bonnard

Between the edge of the afternoon
and dusk, between the bath's white
rim and the band of apricot light,
she bathed, each day, like dreaming.

From the doorway he noted
her right foot hooked for balance
beneath the enamel lip, body
and water all one in a miasma

of mist, a haze of lavender blue.
Such intimacy. A woman, two walls,
a chequered floor, the small
curled dog basking in a pool

of sun reflected from the tiles
above the bath. Outside
the heavy heat. So many times
he has drawn her, caught the obsessive

soaping of her small breasts,
compressed the crouched frame into
his picture space, the nervy movements
that hemmed in his life.

The house exudes her still,
breathes her from each sunlit corner,
secretes her lingering smell
from shelves of rosewood *armoires*,

and the folded silk *chemises*
he doesn't have the heart to touch.
And from the landing, his memory tricks,
as through the open door the smudged

floor glistens with silvered tracks,
her watered foot prints to and from
the tub where she floats in almond oil
deep in her sarcophagus of light.

After Degas

Her young body lies, a twisted S,
on a mattress of cool sand
under the tilted parasol

in the pool of her black skirt,
the encased striations of her pin-
striped blouse. Beneath closed

eye-lids she breathes the thick
smell of surf and shore, hears
the yelp of damp dogs, the distant

shrieks of children running bare-
foot beneath the pewter sky,
as her sodden hair pours

onto the spread white cloth
where her mother drags
and drags the shark-toothed comb

through the ferny tangled mass.
She flinches, surfacing from day-
dreams: fat-bellied sails of distant

ships taut as bare skin, fish-tang
of rigging, the heave and heft
of dripping nets, wind unhooking

her like the steel eyelets on her bodice,
a taste of salt on her lips.

Woodcuts

'Love is not love until love's vulnerable.'
Theodore Roethke

1. *Flowers*

She wakes into forgetfulness
only her body remembering
the bunch-of-five roses decorating
her white arm, the curve of her bare
shoulder, the tattoo of crimson florets
opening into stamens of black.
Petals of purple where his fingers
had pressed into pale flesh.
And still the feel and smell of him –
flared nostrils, the hot spittle at the edge
of his mouth. Fur and skin and hooves.
And she remembers how that first
time he had called her beautiful,
had with those words wiped away
a father's spilt milk of indifference,
until he too could not bear the taste
of her fear, ripping it from her dark soil
like weeds by the roots.
Now she turns into the tattered morning,
sees across the room
he has unzipped his bull-body:
a small slumped boy with terror on his face.

2. *Flood*

His sentences spill like rivers across
her wide plains breaking dried banks.

She is drowning in words.
Tides blue as the morning moon rush in

and in, sheets of thawing ice loosen
like shattered panes of greenhouse glass.

She tries to escape to the safe hilltops
of herself, to sail over cornfields,

the roofs of houses, attics filled
with dead bees and dust, past fish

dangling like paper lanterns phosphorescent
in the topmost branches of elms.

She would drop anchor with him in a green
meadow but the torrent sweeps on,

as her curved keel grazes the tips of ruined vines
where stringy goats once grazed and dolphins

swim among the pines. She would invite
him to share the quite places of herself,

but as she gulps for air, he pours in.
The whole briny force of him.

3. Kitchen Dancing

They have closed the door
leaving her to the cracked cornices,
the junk mail on the mat,
hair like graffiti in marbled cakes
of soap, pork chops congealing
in pools of blood in a polystyrene
pack at the back of the fridge.

She didn't mean to look,
standing in front of the basin,
its polished sentinels of taps –
the foam of her brushed teeth
flecked with threads of crimson –
didn't mean to penetrate that
other brittle gaze, intrude
like a passing stranger's
face on the crowded tube.

Now in the stale morning
among pizza and cold tea-bags,
the debris of other lives,
she strokes her breasts,
her untouched thighs,
throws back her head and
swaying slightly by the sink
slowly stamps out the half-
remembered steps.

4. Morning

Who is this woman
running down the mountain
of morning through the blue-
washed dawn between
the cracked cloches along
puddled paths where dripping
webs of shadow coil
among the glass-house ferns
the spotted orchids
and smeared light speckling
the stagnant pond
where plain carp lurk
beneath the black lily pads?

Who is this running woman
hair lifted like straw
by the light wind,
bleached shadow against
the kitchen-garden wall?
Why has she crept
from the snowy fissures,
the steep mountain
of plain starched sheets
into the chill garden carrying
the imprinted breath of him,
the prod of his ice tongue,
his cold glass kiss?

Alchemies

1. Birmingham Goldsmith

Each morning with a click of bicycle chain
he leaves her at the mangle in the grey backyard
the fire-fly of his fag-end disappearing in the dark
like a hot kiss.

The streets smell of coal-dust and sleep
and Orion is still bedded down behind the gasometer,
as men spill from yellow-throated doorways hunkered
beneath flat caps, dreaming of frowsty sheets.

All day beneath the zircon blue of kerosene
he sits nailed to the wooden bench
by his leather apron spread to catch
the gilt-edged dust that pollens

his skilled fingers saffron
as he buffs and burnishes 9ct curbs
and belcher chains, chaises the bevels
of machine-turned rings for other women's hands.

All morning she heaves grey underwear
from aluminium to windy washing line
wiping suds from raw fingers
onto her flowered apron to wait

for meter-men, agents with rent books
as dogs bark their arrival up the windy alley.
Her back aches. What she needs is sleep
as she pictures him washing the aureate dust

from his sweat-soaked hair, his white body
bent above the pantry sink, wet head
shimmering beneath the kitchen lamp,
Archangel in a halo of gold.

2. The Jeweller's Mistress

At night in her high white bed
she dreams of piercing
his electroplated heart,
annealing its gilded armour
into liquid gold.
In the dark she would burnish
his sharp corners, the soldered seams
that hem him in,
planish and polish with pumice
and fine sand his jagged exterior
on her spinning felt bob,
sink her die like sharp teeth
into his new softness,
engrave her name
across his chest decorating
the chasing with a tattoo
of translucent Champlève
or Baisse-taille, then hallmark
his Millgrain
with her own secret stamp;
a lion passant, behind
the pink whorl of his left ear.

3. The Assayist

Each evening he takes his
small failures, isolating
what was jewel-like, precious,
the topaz slant of winter light
across the dim hall, a drop of rain
patinating a pigeon's wing,
from the day's dark mass,
placing it in a cupel of bone ash
in the furnace's fiery maw.
This is true alchemy,
not mere pinchbeck promises
or the transmutation of fool's gold.

Solids melt. What is base
oxidises, absorbed as if by magic
until it yields a tiny bead
of dull gold. This he will cool,
flatten, roll, boil in nitric acid
to separate impure from pure.
Then he will weigh the residue
balancing the black ash
of midnight against the glint
of dawn, stamp his gleaming
bullion with its carat, an anchor,
three castles, a leopard's head.

4. *The Gold Cutter's Daughter*

That which you weave,
        like Judea's first goldsmith,
                Bezalel, into vineleaves of gold,
                        I wear threaded in my thick dark hair.

Among these damp brick streets,
        these pigeon-coloured days,
                you pierce my coral ear and fix it with
                        a little Gold Star,

so they may know me for what I am
        a stranger. My mouth fills with feathers, a weight
                of foreign words. At night I dream of forests,
                        smell the quiet darkness of snow.

Room in New York, 1932

(after Edward Hopper)

Her dress is red.
Her bare arms white as sour cream.
Her hair is malt and softly looped
behind the long arc of her pale neck.
In the half-shadow she scans the page
of her book, her face the colour
of bruised plums, then sighs and turns
towards the lamp which has a shade
the same faded red as her dress.

His shirt is white.
His buttoned waistcoat and knotted tie
are black. He has taken off his jacket
in the heat and opened the window
onto the sticky night.
He sits in a pink velvet chair,
his face inclined towards his newspaper
as sometimes he might incline it
towards a kiss.

Their bowed heads form
a diagonal across the room,
though her chin is tilted to the right
and his to the left.
There is nothing between them
except a small round maple-wood table
set with a lace cloth. The table is polished
and shimmers like a lake.
But it is not a lake.
It is simply a table that sits
between them, just as the walls,
which are yellow as illness
are just walls.

Somewhere down the hall
a door slams.

Moths

For weeks she has known they
are in there. The furred flutterings
between escarpments of wool,
folded crevices of blankets.

Spring she sprinkled snowballs
of camphor, but still, behind
closed doors imagines clouds
of wood-brown wings beating

between the hills and hummocks
of outgrown sweater, mandibles
shredding their discarded winter warmth.
All summer they must have hatched

in the fierce heat, now slub-laced motes
slip like dust behind her eyelids,
flit across her tea-coloured dreams.
She will not open the cupboard,

let them out to whirr in curtains
and hair towards the bright light
of vacant bedrooms. Again
she will turn away to polish taps,

water the lemon balm,
leave for another day the pale
featherings unravelling her satin trims.

Cooking Fish

Quick as a flash –
under the ventricle fins –
a steel blade piercing wet flesh
mottled as muddied pebbles,
he scrapes out a dark trail
of guts, a mauve heart
like hidden secrets beneath
a twist of clear water
from the cold tap.

Pink flesh pale as the hidden
skin of his groin. Row
of tiny dragon teeth, milk-
white eye, a filmy moon
in the beak of a head, body
curved to the hump of the bridge
where a Chinaman hurries home
among willows of blue –
smell of dark reeds and ponds.

A meal *à deux*.
She poaches it slowly.
stuffs along the spine
with fine feathers of dill,
black pellets of peppercorn,
mushrooms, slivers of garlic sliced
thin as the aorta of her heart
that hisses and hisses
he loves, he loves me not.

Border

Climbing from the bath, all pink-skinned
    and gleaming, she reaches for a towel to wipe
        away the mist from the smeared glass,

and in the pale room's falling light, among
    the brittle shadows of the white tiled room,
        among the lotions and the pills, stands face

to face with a self she hardly knows.
    This is not the woman, half-wrapped in a blue towel,
        a fraction of her left breast exposed,

like the pale crescent of a sickle moon,
    she has woken with each morning
        desire dewy on her night breath.

This is the hour of reckoning. The slow descent
    into that other country where alluvial
        flesh thickens criss-crossed with well-worn tracks,

those scars of stubborn hope.
    Now there is only tomorrow's face,
        caverns and creases filling with dry dust,

as in the dim light she remembers the curve
    of an arm once waiting out-stretched on a crumpled bed;
        a wet mouth opening, that bitter taste of sweat.

Gone to Earth

Finally, one night you slipped in
under my defences,
the chicken wire raised to keep out
foxy dreams – though I had beckoned
before and you had not come.

I found you, in the end, down some
muddy track, fringed with blackberries,
the windows of your car jammed,
each door sealed with gaffer's tape,
the sort of precision you usually
found it hard to muster.

And all around you the blue
was drawing in and in –
wrapping tighter and tighter,
a tourniquet of darkness blotting
out the braille-point stars over
the mounded belly of Salisbury plain,

until you could no longer believe
it would ever end. Then sometime
past midnight, cocooned in a duvet,
you tipped the reclining seat,
turned on the engine and like
a wounded fox, lay down to die…

oh my brother, that we might
have held, for a moment, those
duplicitous stars in our joint gaze
before somewhere across the damp
morning fields the dawn rose,
as it would have anyway.

Books

Amongst 'things found'
a vast plastic bag of books
as if, like that boy-king
with his painted peacock-eye
of kohl, you could fill
that metal tomb, that gas-filled car
with seeds of dormant knowledge
like grains of ancient barley that sprout
centuries after the plunder of grave-dark
to equip you for another better life.
Alchemies and knowledge
that had not served, had
failed you here. As if,
as if you could lay down
pearls, gobbets of wisdom
like dates or carved sardonyx,
blue lapis lazuli set in granulated
beads of gold, rare tinctures or
ointments of myrrh, to be absorbed
through your alabaster skin,
as the night enfolded you,
drew you home across
the dark-green, green-dark
Styx, to where such knowledge
may yield meaning beyond
the hollow howl of words.

Loss

It goes on and on
like the blue-veined rivers
that cross and criss-cross maps
or tracks that coil
along rocky coastal paths
where rabbits' droppings
dry in raisin pellets
between gorse and heather
stunted by salt-filled spray.

It goes on and on
like the trace of an owl's
cry from a distant barn,
feathers and fur
pearl vertebrae of mice
under the rotting straw

endless as the drip
of rain in the high beeches,
the plume of smoke rising
in a coil above the neighbour's
privet, beyond cracked cloches
and stagnant pond, where
leaves gather behind the shed.

Chorus, coda, refrain

Christmas

I try to imagine
if he came back,
pressing his pale half-forgotten

face against the cold pane,
looking in through shadows
of lamplight and rain

at the smeared glasses, the empty
bottles of wine and fallen needles
of Christmas pine.

The deserted street silent
in December dark, the curtains
at each window drawn tight

to stop the bleeding out of private light
and he watching, as we recycle pain,
wondering why, again and again

we don't learn love's declensions.
Yet if he stayed a moment longer
he might find, among the smell

of discarded orange rind,
the odour of unmade beds
and drying sheets, of coal dust,

and yellow chrysanthemums
wilting in a jar, a shifting sense
of what has changed –

dilute as a homeopath's dose
invisible in the pale liquid's glass –
into a glimmer of something

precious: like a lost ring,
a pebble, a rusty key,
a question mark of fallen hair

Darwin's Worms

En masse, they were, he realised,
the earth's natural geologists, noted how
a piece of drained marl

harrowed then ploughed
by the heavy tread of feathered cobs
would disclose beneath its fine tilth,

the soft mulch of vegetable decay,
blue shards of pottery, splinters of ivory bone
ejected at the mouth of castes.

He studied their hermaphrodite matings,
recorded how their work was carried out
hidden beneath the surface geest or at night

under a wet moon as their pink bodies
wandered digesting and ejecting the triturated earth.
All life, he now saw, was informed

by loss, each micro-second
a brief stay against erasure
before invisibility set in.

And then he understood
how he must relinquish redemption,
learn to let time pass and heal,

for what was divinity if it could only come
with a wing-beat of angels?
And in his mind's eye he glimpsed

the grand collaboration, the earth
transformed by their inexhaustible work, reborn
again and again through the intestines of worms.

Hotel

In the hush of hidden rooms where a slit
of lamp-light seeps like a half-forgotten memory
beneath her door and hairballs of dust

gather along the mantle by the unmade bed,
she wraps the lonely night about her
in a shawl.

Along buried phone lines the voices of strangers
weep through paper walls bruised as tender skin,
open mouths inhaling rancid dreams.

Above an old man is sleeping his shameless sleep,
while below the nervous girl in a blue dress
unpacks her invisible face in front

of the hostile glass to place it on a shelf
beside the sample soaps,
the sachets of free shampoo.

Outside the wind and rain
are endless. The night lurks,
a furtive voyeur beneath

the slouching shadows of lamp posts
exhaling its hot breath, as she stands
cheek pressed against the cold pane

watching trams criss-cross the damp city
going somewhere, going nowhere.
Footfalls echo down

silent corridors where pairs of shoes
lie discarded like old loves.
Every journey we make begins and ends

in solitude. Though blood and skin
know that in the secret dark invisible
strangers must breathe in each other's breath.

TIM KENDALL

Eurydice

Although we tried to synchronise our lives,
time still kept slipping by; each dinner date
would find me running fashionably late,
and you'd be long since gone when I arrived.

Too late, too slow. You guessed we couldn't last,
but reconciled the hours we never spent
by quoting Einstein's thought-experiment
to *prove* that living long means living fast.

So now I imagine our final night
laden with heat and a lost romance,
where you, once more, have vanished without trace:

you, blazing away on your beam of light
untroubled, except for a backward glance
to track the wrinkles ploughing through my face.

Astronauts

The earliest astronauts
understood the risks:
they'd always half expected

God to swat
their overreaching craft.
When nothing of note occurred,

they carried back
for analysis
a punnet of blackest space,

which the scientists
laser-blasted to conclude
that God did not exist.

The astronauts' confidence grew.
Soon they were
tailgating comets,

marvelling
that man should be
so impudent, so great.

Amidst the worldwide
carnival, a veteran
began to recall

how he'd felt homesick
not for his little town
nor for his state or nation,

but for a planet
he could blot out
with his thumb.

Tomatoes

Our landlady Mrs Furze occupied the upper half of the house. Her husband had been killed in the war by a direct hit on an air-raid shelter. 'He survived the trenches, and got blown to bits down the Barbican.' And she'd give a little laugh. 'You know, they were wonderful times, the war years. We'd go dancing on the Hoe every week. Open air, hundreds of couples. And not just dancing.' Mrs Furze had a faded pink rinse. She was a kindly woman. Each Sunday I'd bring up her newspaper and sit in the kitchen while she read me the more salacious stories.

My mother got on well with Mrs Furze until they fell out over the tomatoes. I took special pride in the tomato plants we grew in the yard, since I'd been allowed to dig the holes and pack the earth over the roots. Setting off for school on a particularly sunny morning I would single out an almost-ripe tomato, and spend the day anticipating the glories awaiting me at home. Several times the tomato had gone when I got back. My mother finally asked Mrs Furze outright if she knew anything about it. Mrs Furze blazed: 'Nothing to do with me.' And she disappeared upstairs.

A few days later my mother spotted her in the yard popping one of our tomatoes whole into her mouth. After that we picked them green, and left them to ripen on the window-sill. It was my job to turn them, twice a day, towards the sun.

Eggbuckland

Joe – it must have been – explained the word.
Some Norman knight, Heker, or Hega, or whatever
(Joe was never hot on names)
had been rewarded with a hamlet
for slaughtering his share at Hastings.
Heker's Book Land, d'you see, which somewhere
down the centuries acquired a church or two,
the necessary inns, a confusion of rickety shacks
for the yokels – in sum, all the trappings
a village ever wants or needs. Then Plymouth overspilled
its banks, and everything got tarmacked.

Not *quite* everything, I might have pointed out,
now that my parents' scrimping
had delivered us from the grime of Keyham
and its incessant dockyard hooter.
Here were fields, even horses, and I quickly
found a slowworm – Joe was all for killing it,
and couldn't believe when I picked it up.
Here was a patch of four-leaved clover,
and eighty-foot trees designed, it seemed, for climbing
where I'd sit and gaze astonished at the views –
as far as Dartmoor, with its nobbly tors.

Here were roads so quiet we played football
in the streets, and chicken too – we'd dart
our bikes in front of screeching cars.
Once I misjudged, the gas van clipped my wheel,
and I ended sprawled across the bonnet.
Joe was so impressed, I became his number two
in the toughest meanest gang for miles.
(There were no other gangs, of course.)
Joe would boast of his exploits with girls,
though the only ones I knew he knew
turned away, indifferent, when we stopped to chat.

Until, that is, the cousin of a junior member
came to stay – just thirteen, but already
graced with legs like compasses.
She seemed intrigued when Joe and I
whizzed downhill, hands outstretched, exhilarated,
yelling something from *Die Fledermaus*
as we belted past her auntie's home.
Die Fledermaus, our anthem, an idea of Joe's
he never properly discussed. Joe pronounced it [dai].
Before long, he was sharing with the gang, *sotto voce*,
what he and she had done on midnight trysts.

I didn't have the heart, or nerve, to tell
she'd seen me walking past alone one day
and rushed outside 'to keep me company'.
How we'd strolled for hours, liking each other,
no frills, no pretence, but comfortable at being ourselves,
and she'd announced she hated Joe, he seemed
such a puppy dog, always boundy, eager to impress.
How soon we were trying our first proper kiss,
tenderly clumsy, I can still recall.
How we'd understood; touched hands and smiled,
then said goodbye for good.

After that I bided time, and watched Joe carefully.
I saw how vulnerable he was, open to attack.
So, I might suggest a visit to the graveyard –
our favourite haunt (our favourite joke) – and sense his fear
when I placed a penny on a grave, and skipped around
a dozen times plus one, all the while

reciting paternosters in a chant. He'd back away
as if a claw might shoot out any second
for its offering. He was trying to laugh,
but I saw the other members watching him,
and watching me, and working out their sums.

Then came the insights of the batty woman,
who lived alone at the end of the street.
we'd all call round from time to time, apple-pie smiles,
politeness every other word, and stuff as many
biscuits as we could, while she rattled on
about lay-lines, astral planes, and something called I-Ching.
Once I was explaining how I loved being asleep,
because I always controlled my dreams, and conjured up
elaborate delights. This became momentous.
She proclaimed I was a psychic, mystical, that sort of thing,
a one-off, one-in-a-million phenomenon.

So began the ouija board, usually in Joe's garage,
and I'd innocently push the glass around
whatever answers people seemed to want to hear –
or what I wanted them to hear. This was my domain.
Joe was told he'd hang at twenty-one, or marry Nicky
(the ugly one) who lived next door, and end up dead of syphilis.
While I would be a great success, a daring jewel thief
who'd never once get caught, and hobnob with the stars.
But when the spirit spelt I too would marry N-I-C-K-Y
I caught Joe off his guard, and forced his head down
in the dirty oil-tray, accusing him of pushing.

Afterwards the gang fell into faction-fights, ambushes,
and finally a truce, whereby we decreed
that Joe and all his hangers-on should pass unkicked
provided their behaviour followed certain codes.
It didn't matter much, because within a year
my parents were looking to move again,
and anyway, the splinter group had lost its bad intent.
Last time I saw Joe, he was outside our house, snooping
round the removal van with that ponderous mug of his.
I hid behind the curtains. 'Joe!' I shouted, 'Joe! Joe!'
Joe jerked his head from side to side, frantically keeping time.

Trajectories

I

I might have dropped my tea, or forgotten
how to rewire a plug – *You educated bunch*,
he'd always gruffle, *no common sense*.
Remember the man who never ducked

and knew he was safe if he heard the shell,
till at last one boomeranged back: not a scratch,
just the relentless gob of blood
treacling out through burst nostrils.

II

More dream than real, more real than dream
Here, you said, *look here*. A child again,
I touched the scar they carved in your neck,

the buds of wings in the curve of your back,
and pictured you, resplendent, as the light
uplifted every perfect feather.

Bread and Butter

I'd buttered her up like a true gastronome
as we strolled slowly back, but once home

she whirled out of reach, demanding to be fed.
I ran downstairs, buttered two slabs of bread,

and returned with the plate to find her
au naturel, reclined like an otter

on my bed, having made of her belly a table.
A golden delicious perched on her navel.

She gestured me over…I noticed as she munched
how the crumbs would nestle in her rolls of paunch

and heard my mother's voice: *It's polite*
to take what's offered. Handed on a plate.

So what was to stop me snaffling the crumbs
like a destitute Hansel, greedy for home?

Hieroglyphs

I dream you, and you come to me
intact, in focus, indiscreet, mouthing
the sweetest lies as if we cared.

As if, in fact, we might begin again
with needle-tracks and scratches down your arms
that might have told in drunken hieroglyphs

how heavy-shouldered I pick my way
through a night of empty forecourts,
back to the etceteras of passion:

the obligatory pathos of discarded shoes,
the glass of water juddering by the bed,
the face my heavenly eyes avoid.

Assignation

Where paths cross and double-cross,
tonight the regular conjunction.

A fumble of hands, silent mouthings,
and always the buttons' rigmarole –

an ebb before impediments
release to sesames of flesh.

Far off, in the city's glare,
guiltless lives lock themselves away.

Here, names escape their faces.
The moon's tremendous search-light

silvers an empty-mouthed cat,
the hedgerows and ruffled fields,

the slow, mesmeric sway of trees
unleaving gently in the autumn breeze.

Perspective

Earlier civilisations
lacked a certain nous
when it came to comets,
eclipses, electrical storms,
frog-showers and other such
dramas of the heavens.

This is the age
of quarks and neutrinos,
of telescopes spinning
to the corners of space
in search of the last enigmas.
There is no stopping us.

I've even heard of a people
whose leading brains
refute the miraculous
by concocting nigh-on
impossible sums
then solving for x and y.

Mystic

I glimpsed God once,
or something very like.

A starry starry night
back in '88 or '9

found me – as usual
tipsy but not drunk –

staring out to sea
and wondering which waves

would break and which would lap.
I'd spend hours doing that.

suddenly the sky
exploded – or so it seemed –

like a city with power restored.
I only understood

a contour, never fixed,
an after-image on the eye,

indelible. Indelible
like the exquisite

sense of loss at homecoming,
like the exile's rage

I'd very soon appreciate.
Since when, nothing, nothing

but silence, infinite
and subtle in its shades.

Mammals

Otter

If I were to mention otters
one would dodge the traffic
and slip silently up to my door.

All I would know of it
would be the whisperings of neighbours
and crumbling spraint on the concrete.

Harvest Mouse

All morning the blackberries bloat in the sun.
Bewildered by their sweetness,
we gorge like many-handed gods.

Against a cobalt sky this afternoon
a single berry quivering at the weight
will slowly free its juices, cell by cell.

Badger

Past midnight a crash of bins
our neighbour's dog barking
and our neighbour shouting.

I remembered the hedgehog
we found last month
unzipped in the long grass.

Ecce Homo

I

Masaccio,
dead at twenty-six,
already understood

that subtleties of dust,
no more, quicken
our corpses with breath.

How else to comprehend
his *Trinity*, where
Christ the life in death

hangs tautened, as if
continuing to fight,
while the Madonna,

wall-faced,
incriminates us all
with her superior air:

see what you've done.
Yes, we kept going back,
but not for guilt.

What drew us
was a skeleton
entombed beneath the Cross:

I was once as thou
art now; as I am now
so wilt thou be.

II

And suddenly
I'm breathing the foetor
of Sicilian catacombs,

with their rag and bone
like low-budget effects.
After fifteen years

I'm witnessing
the olive-skinned,
translucent girl

who sleeps the centuries
awaiting
her sword-tongued Christ.

And I'm pondering the formula –
prohibited, then lost –
to incorrupt the flesh.

Imagine: I take
a syringe, so, and probe
our one flesh for a vein.

Arno

A brood of coypus
by the Ponte Vecchio –
our honeymoon gift.

Nocturnal

The fox revolves its frozen circuits
then slows, to nuzzle a breeze.
A birdless moonless sky, split only
by the silent flicker and swerve
of a bat, sweeping the frequencies.
Flushed in the fire's afterglow, you turn
and settle with the silhouettes.

No sound disturbs your sleep.
No owl, no engine ticking over.
Traffic lights change for empty streets.
The river stumbles, holds,
glazed with intricate designs,
as the Earth pursues our smooth
rotation to the light.

Fugue

At last he loses himself
far above time, where occasional

breaks in the cloud reveal
cities compressed into microchips

and car-specks
pursuing irrelevant ends.

Fear never follows so high,
but seeps through his nights

to the instant he steps off the plane,
almost papal with gratitude.

Always the frisson
where fear begins.

Seven, I'd be, or thereabouts,
on the climbing-frame's

highest rung, while the girl next door
shouted to jump:

go on, it's easy.
And because she was pretty, I jumped.

Sarah, her name, Sarah.
She caught cabbage-whites in her net

and squeezed their heads for a penny a time.
I begged her, no, please no.

Like dust, she'd say, look, no blood.
She herself, dead in a year, maybe two.

The fear of his dreams was
never the casual decline

where passengers scream
or scream their Hail Marys.

Never the death
expected and rehearsed,

but the unlooked-for,
the obliterating instant.

As it was in the beginning,
where memory starts

or a story mistaken for memory.
Of wanting to taste the butterflies,

their reds, their blues and their whites,
as they flittered just beyond reach,

and I forgot my mother
until the whoosh whoosh in waves

as she lifted me
up out of the pond

to explosions of light.
Her extravagant wound,

welling with blood.
Then later the scar,

close to beige
which — even today — she still covers up.

Two chances, his mother would say,
for interviews or prizes or asking a girl out

or anything at all, you got two chances.
Only now, released above cloud,

above dreams, he understands
the furtive ecstasies of fear.

Only now, and once before, that winter
on Etna, shivering in the sun.

I squinted down a crater, expecting
something like a cauldron, witches' brew,

but glimpsed whole cities engulfed
by eruptions of snow.

Heat death — big freeze, big crunch,
he never could decide,

though sometimes he plumped
for a sennet of trumpets

to laud an arrival, the promise fulfilled.
He sensed how the soil

would shift and erupt with a strange new bud
which sprouts in profusion

everywhere
as eager flesh comes fighting for air.

And perhaps, yes, in my grandmother's garden,
where I'd dig for pottery

and kneel for hours, trying to match the shards.
Dozens of patterns, and hardly ever

the same one twice, though always I hoped
to recreate the pots, piece by shattered piece.

And here, far above time. Above time
or at least, a different time,

where atomic clocks can detect
the requisite miracle blip.

A matter of nanoseconds
smudging the present,

smudging the fear
as a life might touch down

safely
at some indefinable point…

Chocolate

Aztecs used cocoa beans as currency;
attending countless wives,
the chiefs would fortify themselves
with flagons of *xocolatl*.

Voltaire drank dozens of cups a week,
and would surely have agreed
with his own Pangloss, who considered
the New World's gift of syphilis
a paltry price to pay
for such unadulterated bliss.

These things get carried too far –
or so I thought, until late last night
when the pair of us snuggled right in,
with our mugs of creamy chocolate
giving up their ghosts.

The Return

You wouldn't forget the grass snake
which slid under my foot for shelter,
the time we tasted sloes, breathed the ramson-reek

and stepped across vistas of sunlight,
and, Clive, you were there,
with unsuspecting months to wait

for the coffin-lid to shut, shut tight
on all your broken synapses – their failure
a junction at midnight –

and after midnight I sit and rock
and drink and see the spider
abseil down the wall, then scurry back.

Divorce

He intends to write of his parents' divorce.

He remembers the view of the sea, and the rock vanishing at high tide. He is four years old. He owns a container of coins with pictures of ships, Spanish galleons. He strokes them and afterwards his hands smell of rust. Coins cold on his tongue. He feels the feel of swallowing one, the feel all the way down.

He intends to write of his parents' divorce. He knows the legends. Footprints in the car – on the seats, and even the ceiling, was it? A hand through glass to reach a lock. Glass in the hallway, and blood.

He locks himself in the bathroom, but only by accident, and his parents are calling. The door almost bursts. He washes his hands, they smell of rust.

He remembers the rock. It looms, it shrinks, a white fist, then there's nothing, really.

REBECCA ELSON

(1960–1999)

An Extract from the Journal
(in course of transcription)

1 an angel come in the form of a fly to take my radiation with me, crawling & hopping on the lead cutouts of my lungs, a small living company

2 how it feels to be a photographic plate of the Universe, full of galaxies being scanned, the xray machine, like a telescope, and me bathed in xrays, like standing space in front of a pulsar spraying xrays into its sky

3 the parable of the Colombian bull. There were frogs, with other frogs on their backs hopping through the tufty snow cropped grass, and they seemed to be the only life...

Aug 12

A smallish room with planes of yellow-amber walls, and doors that open & close letting in sounds of televisions & tea trollies, and always the hum & beep of things. Outside the venetian slats across the window, Cambridge is baking in an un-English sun. This morning there were swallows filling the air outside this 10th floor room. And now, nothing moving, & no sounds, so that even when an airplane drifts across the sky, it makes no sound, & doesn't really seem to move. Hard to concentrate, hard to get out of the reality of drips & tubes & polished linoleum & into something more large & beyond, & sustaining & deep.

Aug 17

Those small cells already hiding out
In the Aladdin's cave of your bones

And those small cells already
Lighting their fires
In the genie caves of my bones

And the blood sowing its seed   its red seed
In the dark earth of my bones

Oct 10

Coming home from the hospital
Taxi, warm air, lights Albinoni
Dangerous closeness of the world

And the bones of the sea
Parched and shivering

...

The childless mother
       (sometimes I feel like a)

hedgerows full of sloes & rosehips

Oct 23

In this upstairs room the sun casts its lace shadow
On one corner wall, scrolling down the lace curtain
Against the muslin, making a puppet show of lace birds

Here I position myself like a cat in the sun, in the warmth
Preening myself, pampering, and sending away other
Things which cats don't have, like fear of the future

Yesterday, planted fifteen snowdrops to bloom in February
By the shed, where I will see them, hanging out the laundry
Some frosty morning in a transparent sun.

Planted a Japanese maple which will grow slowly,
Gracefully, with its deep red leaves against the fence.
That we might find stillness by its side, in its small shade.

Planted a cherry tree on centre stage, to grow large
And abundant with sweet red fruit that the birds will try to eat
And why not, they too deserve sweetness for their singing.

Planted a forsythia to bloom like sunshine in March,
Caught in the corner of your eye on an impenetrably grey day
A small illusion to grow larger every spring

And planted a flowering currant, company for the forsythia,
To hold a twig between thumb and forefinger, its blossoms
Bending down, and lift them over and over to smell.

All this awaiting spring, anticipating, hoping, planning
Against small cruel voices which tease in the night
About last Christmases & last springs, flowers blooming without you.

Like reserving a place for the spectacle of spring
An autumn & a winter still to traverse.

August on Ward C10

The door swinging open & closed & open & closed
Ladies in pink offering tea
Blue checked nurses come for blood, come with small cups of pills
I lie in a narrow bed, cooperative,
My body going to bones
In the shower, my skin & bones body almost too light to stand
And shivering with nothing to protect it, all in the airconditioned
August cool.

The doors swings open & closed
My mother in her summer skirt, her bag full of books & Marks &
                                                    Spencer food
And A. with his plaster cast ankle, his crutches leaning on the wall
Another night gone, with rattling wheels of the drip stand
And the alarm bells going off & on
And the thick disinfectant smells.

Coming & going they complain of heat outside
Though in room 1 there is airconditioned cool
They come in putting on sweaters, coughing a dry cough
On the news on television, the drought goes on

The hottest summer in a hundred years
And the door swings open and closed.

Oct 27

This town...
Wind catches you through the shopping mall
Spitting rain and cold and you have to
Hunch your shoulders against it
And the fat girls & flying wrappers
Somewhere, you have to tell yourself
There are great thoughts percolating up
Like snowdrops, preparing for spring.
And in candlelight under the great vaults
The small boys have let go the first soaring note
Of evensong, shivering your spine
But against these cloistered rarities
Is the deadliness of high street shops
The mediocre uniformity of risks
Of blue-legged schoolgirls without socks
Of a market full of apples in small
Brown paper bags, no ample generosity
This is what we can carry, this is all.
If you're lucky, bells will start to peal
Out of a blue winter night
And the sun will make an effort at a sunset
And if you are paid, and part of the great pursuits
Then you might feel pleased with your day's labours
But if you have only been blown through
The shopping mall with empty wrappers
And fat girls with their coats flying open
Then god help you when you come home
To try & discover the meaning of this or
Any other dwelling, things to undo
And things to do over again
And over again.
Search for the miracles and beauty all around
It is not hard to find something to make
You bow your head with gratitude.

Dec 17 Pescara

Outside the figs like sculptures against a grey sky
A few dry figs clinging to their skins

A few rotting grapes sagging like old breasts
In clusters from their vines
The windows wet with condensation
And always the bells
These are sleeping times, peaceful, here in this haven
At the bottom of the garden
Upstairs the others come and go
And grandmother twisted with the same anger,
Emptiness, frustration of a life not lived
Or lived in kneeling, praying, serving
Each one of us a god, a spirit, angel
To be served, each one to serve
To be ushered into the world and out again
Biting our anger like a stick
The dry splinters filling our mouths,
And spit out in a moment of forgetting
The sanctity of all our souls, fearing death
Who lives, who forgets, who dies miserably and young
There are rough-skinned pomegranates still on their branch
I have almost forgotten the universe already
Though sometimes, before sleep, it presents itself again
In diagrams awaiting an interpretation
In an inconsistency or in a proof
Some dry force returning inward, some need
Some other's anguish over wasted minutes
Of a life not fully lived, the panic racing towards the finishing line
Exhausted but not wanting the end
No glory, no prize, but there will be time,
The lights going down, snow, someone else's snow
A yearning for family, not to be the one left out
The one missing at the dinner table
As

Dec 22

New gods gathering slowly like a storm.
Like paper, bark slipping from the trees
Like elephants, branches broken in the sand
Like wires, eels swimming in the mud
And all the things that wash up on the shore
Shells & crabs & finally, sun,

You two loves, do not let the tide go out
You old man, fishing with your high boots,
You others, talking in the shelter of a wall
Toothless with mischief, with wisdom, with what?
What's left of the spirit of this town
Where grown men spend their days tipping truckloads of rocks
Into the sea, and watching the bleached heap
Grow long, nod their heads in progress,
Smoking another cigarette, butt in the sand
While an old man stands low on the beach
Shaking his head saying how unnatural it is
The sea castrated, waves calmed to murmurs,
How you can't see the horizon anymore
Just bleached mountain boulders
Going back to the sea unnaturally
Where's the love of earth, the mystery
In acquisition, coats & boots
How they judge you by the cost of your hat,
The flow of your hair
What moves you? What lifts you up above yourself
Where do you go to pray
To feel the gods rising inside you
Your otherliness, like candle heat, like peace.

...

Breakwater

Old man standing on the beach, at this feet
Castrated sea, sad like an old dog
Twitching in his sleep
Saying, can't see the horizon anymore
Just a ridge of stones a hundred yards off shore,
Grown men with their cigarettes their trucks
Tipping pale mountain rocks into the sea
And all the waves stubbed out.

...

Jan 1 (Scanno)

First of the year up a valley
With a long view
Cloud, sun, cloud
Cropped grass, white stones
A river of sheep, sharp wind
A sheltering stone,
A spring bubbling out from some secret place
And we stopped to bless ourselves
Asking for compassion
Move always towards what you love
Move towards what you have always loved
Air clear, air still, edging of stone against stone
Under boot
Elsewhere the year coming in slowly
Lake waves lapping on the stone.

Jan 2

Low clouds hanging still above Frattura
Above the lake
And we take the back roads between the pines
Soft brown meadows, waiting for snow
Miraculous, and close
Valleys dropping out of mist, opening
In the town, an old woman dressed in black
Climb the stepped streets to the tower
Looking down the slit of turquoise lake
Here at last there is air to breathe.
A cloud lifts itself behind a pine
Two birds. Runes of vacant trees
Feel your muscles again, & lungs
Living with the mountains
Imagine how it must feel, these roots creeping into you,
Mother of all, a falling rock scratching, bruising
And long brooks running off your back
Eating sky, waiting for snow, waiting

Jan 4

Two days now, smooth silver crests
A blue, blue sky, warm sun
Wind worn stones beneath your boots
Tramping over the highest places of the soul
Of joy, the blue sky flooding your bones
There, the tiny sheep flowing towards the valley floor
In rivulets around the boulders, dogs
There, a winding road shouldering a hill
There, the new snow shining on a peak.
Let there never be a time when these
Are far from my present, my mind.
On the darkest day of English grey
A goat is leaping up this hillside
Uproarious with light.

Feb 6

A month now, doing things always
Cold grey, days like black & white photos
Cracked, no joy hardly, river drained
To mud & rubbish, swans edged back
Each morning this: open the curtain
Pampas grass blowing in the garden
Head wind, tail wind, always grey
Cold like punishment slapping your face.
At work, a deep square of space
So endless you could fall forever
So many galaxies, so many people gone
And yet to come
And simply, we go on planning things
And eating lunch.
I swim among them in the afternoon
And come to know them all
And this way they take your mind like dark fish
Like transparent things that slide through the deepest oceans
Sleep on the bottom where there is no bottom,
In the great deep rifts.
Some days there is one of me, so unthinkably unique
So perishable, so tragic in its passage

Some days I am just a step from somewhere
To somewhere else. A light step, well sprung
And happy in the taking
I count stars, contradict hypotheses
But it is for the looking of these spots arranged
And tinted with age, with chemistry
How metals glow red & our blue
Combustion solves nothing
And the great eye goes on winking
Open & shut & open & shut & swallowing
Bits of space & spitting them out in our monitors
It is all looking really, that is the pleasure
And inventing what might look the same
And calling it understanding
And all of that keeps back the fear
So you only catch a glimpse of it from time to time
Like an old woman parting a lace curtain just an inch
To see.

May 3

Oh garden, oh our earth
Storming with dry winds
Over your new barrenness
No more tenderness towards seeds

May 19

Like running
Like looking through oceans
Mapping the strange, transparent fish
In that rubber round of space

Poem for a Wedding 1   To a Travelling Companion

These promises we speak
Indulgence, forgiveness, respect
Love hard as stone
Let us never lose
May we
Now in the warm sun

Splendid, tremendous, pangs
Even when the road bends into shadow
Torrents, certainty
Palms upwards
In the year of our birth
Delivered into the world
And having rounded all obstacles
Stepping closer
Our separate childhoods, adventures
Like two growing things
Never to cower or lean or demand
Never to be taken for granted
Diving into a cold lake
To take with thanks the outside & the new
I take you to my heart
All the time ahead of us
And all the world

Travelling Companions

In the year of our birth,
Me at apogee, in a new world
The snow directionless and mute,
You at perigee & hot & brown
In your ancestral olive grove
With all its waiting gods,
We took the road.

You at seven, watching the girl
      Through the garden fence,
Your heart flapping like doves;
Me by a forest lake
Each minnow a flash of joy
You in a foreign city, notebook & pen
Bound for an expanse not crossed by signs;
Me in some departure lounge
Gone for the weight of green,
A universe still young, still warm.

We met, one moving faster, passing
Met again, shared water, bread
The miracle of our unmated hearts
And passed, and met again
And this time, falling into step.

You honour me this voyage
You & your sweet soul
And me, lucky as clover,
As stars.

May 26

Who is to say what a flower feels
On opening its most secret heart
To a disinterested sky

That those who marry in hope
Are simply more naïve
Than those who marry in desperation
Or despair

This saxon soul   This my saxon soul
This salt of its diet, grief   My salt, my grief

Nostalgia, aching

The law of the universe is that anything possible will happen
You turned out to be possible so you happened

June 8
Poem for the Second Born

– being left out
not being celebrated
an ordinary miracle
still, the sister who has gone before
no Pandora
no mystery
sooner or later though
an older sister   snapping at flies
                                    in a still heat

Instructions to Myself

Country diary. Saturday, June 8

Mossa chases butterflies in the meadow
Discovers the nymph Echo
And is enchanted, or disturbed
Run in the meadow, discover sleeping
Places of four deer, Mossa long gone
Chasing
Church bell from up the hill
Ringing 6, hot still
Swimming in the soft silty pond
Goldfish slipping away

June 9

Swallowing the stars as an antidote
to fearing death
spiky, luminous   bright & spiky stars
These & other antidotes to death
Swallowing also the dark sky

Antidotes To Fearing Death

Long & elegant ancestral bones
Bright & spiky stars

Time's long reach
An earth that goes on spinning
A boat in this moment
This summer afternoon
Drifting on a loose
Shade-rimmed pond
Water snake slipping over pond weed
Frogs dangling their hind legs
Deep into silty opalescence
Pollen closing the surface
Dragonflies skimming back & forth
Small dragonflies small lizards

Country Diary June 9
Sunday heat, siesta time
Manana howling with
Pride over a caught
Lizard iridescent green
Angry. Lifted head
Small toothless dinosaur
teasing pawed cat
Mossa chasing butterflies
Because there are no lions

A dog our companion
In this same place there was
A deep swamp with dragonflies
Loud, enormous, a reptile
Like a tree raising its head
Like a fern uncurling from
The depths.

With some permissive phase
of evolution, ourselves seeming
large & powerful, our reptilian
past shrunken to small & harmless memories.